T0150920

INTRODUCTION

---◆---

Dinosaurs ruled the Earth for more than 150 million years, but until about 200 years ago, no one knew they existed. People had been digging up huge bones for thousands of years, but they thought they belonged to dragons or mythical monsters. It was only in the 1820s that scientists figured out that these fossilized bones belonged to enormous, extinct reptiles.

Fossils of dinosaur footprints, eggs, nests, teeth, and dung (called

→ **GO TO PAGE 31 FOR THE PROTOCERATOPS**

→ **GO TO PAGE 33 FOR THE ARCHAEOPTERYX**

coprolites) were also discovered, and these gave scientists clues as to how these creatures lived. Footprints showed how large they were, whether they lived in groups, and if they dragged their tails. Eggs and nests explained how they raised their young, and teeth and dung revealed what they ate.

Around 65 million years ago, there were dramatic volcanic eruptions in what is now India. Tons of ash and dust blasted into the air, blocking heat and light from the Sun. At about the same time, a huge meteorite hit the Earth off the coast of Mexico, causing tidal waves and fires and throwing even more debris into the atmosphere. Without sunlight, plants couldn't survive, and three-fourths of living things, including the dinosaurs, were wiped out.

AGE OF THE DINOSAURS

The Mesozoic Era lasted from 245 to 65 million years ago (mya). It is divided into three periods:

Triassic (245–213 mya)
Jurassic (213–144 mya)
Cretaceous (144–65 mya)

The Cretaceous period ended with a mass extinction. Almost all creatures died, but the small mammals that lived alongside the dinosaurs survived and grew bigger. The age of dinosaurs was over and the age of mammals had begun.

MUSICAL HEADGEAR

PARASAUROLOPHUS *(pa-roh-sore-OLL-off-us)*

Parasaurolophus' most striking feature was its huge crest. At first, scientists thought it might be a snorkel, a weapon, or a tool to push branches out of the way. Now they think it was used to make a noise. When air is blown through the crest, it sounds like a trombone, so Parasaurolophus probably used it to communicate with other members of the herd. The largest males would have made the loudest noise. This sound would have attracted females and also scared rivals away. The skull of a large male Parasaurolophus was as long as a fully grown human.

 LIVED: 76–74 million years ago

 PERIOD: Late Cretaceous

 LENGTH: up to 33 feet

 DIET: horsetails, ginkgoes, pine needles, and other low-growing plants

 NAME MEANS: "like Saurolophus" because it looks like another crested dinosaur called Saurolophus

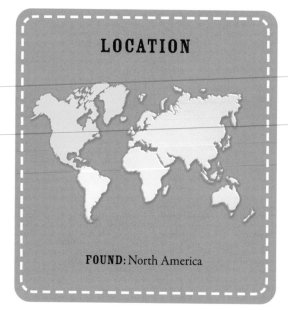

Parasaurolophus often walked on four legs,
but probably ran on two to escape predators.
It was able to sprint at 25 miles an hour
so it could have outrun a T. rex.

LOCATION

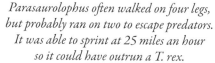

FOUND: North America

DID YOU KNOW...?

❓ Parasaurolophus was a hadrosaur—a family of duckbilled dinosaurs known for their distinctive head crests. Females had smaller crests than males, and a fossilized skin impression shows that they had pebbly scales.

❓ Like humans, Parasaurolophus voices got deeper as they grew! Fossils of inner ears and crests show that young Parasaurolophus made higher sounds.

❓ Parasaurolophus had hundreds of tiny teeth. As they wore down, front teeth were replaced with new teeth from the back.

LONG-FANGED HUNTER

CERATOSAURUS *(Ser-RAT-uh-sore-us)*

Ceratosaurus was a powerful predator with long, bladelike teeth for slicing through the flesh of its prey. It lived alongside other meat-eating dinosaurs, such as Allosaurus and Torvosaurus, and it probably avoided clashes with these other bigger beasts by feeding on different prey. Ceratosaurus teeth are often found in wetland areas, so it may have hunted water-based prey such as lungfish and small crocodiles. Ceratosaurus had a flexible and muscular tail that might have helped with balance and speed when it was running and fighting, or perhaps even swimming.

 LIVED: 156–144 million years ago

 PERIOD: Late Jurassic

 LENGTH: up to 23 feet

 DIET: smaller dinosaurs and reptiles, and possibly fish and turtles

 NAME MEANS: "horned lizard" because of the horn on its snout

The short horn on Ceratosaurus' nose was not strong enough for fighting, so it was probably used for display.

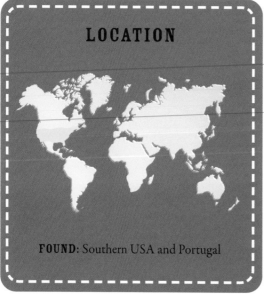

LOCATION

FOUND: Southern USA and Portugal

DID YOU KNOW...?

❓ Several dinosaur fossils have been found bearing Ceratosaurus tooth marks. It was probably a scavenger as well as a hunter.

❓ Ceratosaurus had a row of bony plates along its spine. These may have been a defense against predators.

❓ Although Ceratosaurus and Allosaurus look similar, Ceratosaurus had four fingers on each hand and Allosaurus had three, which shows that they are not as closely related to each other as they might seem.

SPEEDY LITTLE HUNTER

COELOPHYSIS *(seal-OH-fie-sis)*

Coelophysis was one of the first meat-eating dinosaurs, but it was far from the top of the food chain. The top predators in the Late Triassic epoch were large reptiles that looked like crocodiles. Although this little therapod (meat-eating, two-legged dinosaur) lived about 200 million years ago, we know a lot about its life because a bone bed containing thousands of Coelophysis fossils was found in a quarry in New Mexico, USA. Paleontologists think that a large group had gathered—perhaps to feed—and were killed by a catastrophic event, such as a flash flood.

 LIVED: 220–190 million years ago

 PERIOD: Late Jurassic

 LENGTH: up to 9 ¾ feet

 DIET: insects, fish, and small reptiles

 NAME MEANS: "hollow form" because of its hollow bones, which made it very light so it could run fast

Coelophysis had powerful back legs, which helped it to catch its fast-moving prey and escape from its enemies.

LOCATION

FOUND: Southern USA, South Africa, and Zimbabwe

DID YOU KNOW...?

❓ Coelophysis has traveled into space! In 1998, a Coelophysis skull was taken on the Endeavour Space Shuttle mission to the Mir Space Station.

❓ Coelophysis had really big eyes and a skeleton much like a bird.

❓ Palaeontologists once thought that Coelophysis ate its own young. Further research showed that it was not a cannibal but ate small reptiles.

PRIMITIVE PREDATOR

HERRERASAURUS *(her-rer-ruh-SORE-us)*

--- --- ◆ --- ---

One of the early large meat-eating dinosaurs, Herrerasaurus was far from the biggest hunter around at the time. Giant reptiles Fasolasuchus and Saurosuchus were the largest predators in Argentina during the Late Triassic. Although they were too slow to chase Herrerasaurus, they probably lay in wait, hoping to ambush it. Herrerasaurus preyed on smaller, plant-eating reptiles, such as Rynchosaurs, which had a parrotlike beak and looked like a cross between a pig and an armadillo. Herrerasaurus used its flexible, sliding lower jaw to hold on to its prey.

 LIVED: 231–225 million years ago

 PERIOD: Late Triassic

 LENGTH: 10 feet

 DIET: plant-eating reptiles

 NAME MEANS: "Herrera's lizard" because Victorino Herrera found its fossil by chance in 1959

Herrerasaurus had a long, narrow skull packed with dozens of serrated teeth for cutting and tearing the flesh of its prey.

LOCATION

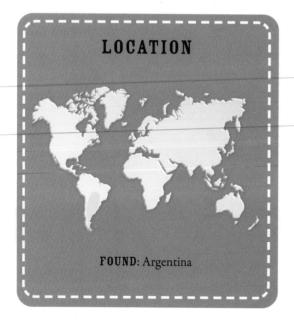

FOUND: Argentina

DID YOU KNOW...?

❓ Herrerasaurus roamed the Earth in the Triassic period when there weren't too many other dinosaurs around. It is one of the earliest dinosaurs to have been found so far.

❓ Herrerasaurus had four toes on its hind feet. This makes it different from many other carnivorous dinosaurs, which had three toes.

❓ Herrerasaurus' forearms moved a lot like a modern pigeon's—they even folded up! They are probably an early example of what would eventually evolve into bird wings.

BONE-CRUSHING KILLER JAWS

TYRANNOSAURUS REX
(tie-RAN-uh-sore-us rex)

Tyrannosaurus rex was one of the largest predators to have walked the Earth. This meat-eating, two-legged killing machine was heavier than an African elephant and as tall as a house. Its huge jaws were over three feet long, and it would use them to grab prey and shake it to death. Tyrannosaurus rex's teeth grew to around 8 inches long, and if it lost one, a new tooth would grow slowly in its place. The teeth of meat-eating dinosaurs such as T. rex continued to grow and be replaced throughout their lives.

 LIVED: 68–66 million years ago

 PERIOD: Cretaceous

 LENGTH: 40 feet

 DIET: other dinosaurs, alive or dead

 NAME MEANS: *Tyrannosaurus* is Greek for "cruel lizard" and *rex* is Latin for "king"

T. rex killed its prey with crushing bites from its powerful jaws. It used its long, sawlike teeth to slice through flesh and crunch through bone.

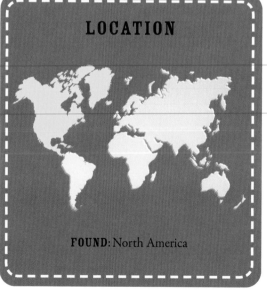

LOCATION

FOUND: North America

DID YOU KNOW...?

❓ T. rex could have eaten as much as 450 pounds of meat and bone in a single bite —that's like eating a large deer in one gulp!

❓ T. rex could not chew. It would bite off chunks of flesh, toss them in the air and let them slide straight down its neck.

❓ A T. rex bite probably had the force of about 1.5 tons—that's like having the weight of a pickup truck behind each tooth!

BIG BRAIN

STENONYCHOSAURUS *(sten-ON-ik-uh-sore-us)*

- - - - ◆ - - - -

Dinosaurs were remarkable for many reasons, but they are not known for their intelligence. Stenonychosaurus had a brain much bigger than most and it was about as smart as a modern-day bird. Apart from its intelligence, Stenonychosaurus had two other weapons to help it catch its prey. Huge, forward-facing eyes allowed it to pinpoint its victims, while a light body and long legs meant it could outrun most animals. These intelligent hunters may even have worked together in packs to bring down larger dinosaurs.

 LIVED: 76–70 million years ago

 PERIOD: Late Cretaceous

 LENGTH: up to 8 feet

 DIET: small mammals and lizards but possibly plants as well

 NAME MEANS: "narrow claw lizard" because the first fossils found had large toe claws

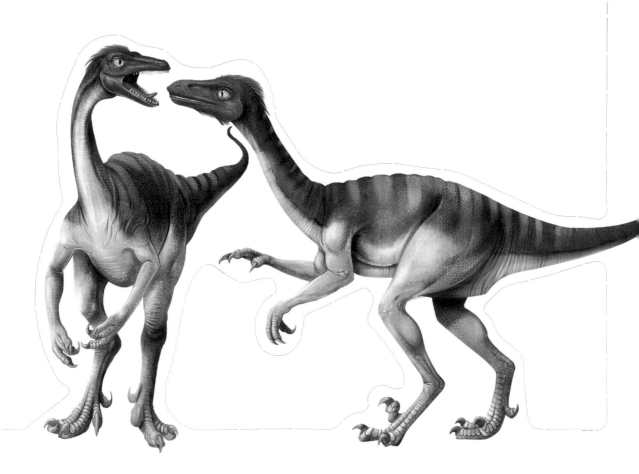

Stenonychosaurus had large, sickle-shaped claws on its second toes that it raised off the ground when it was running.

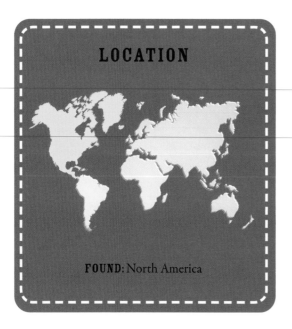

LOCATION

FOUND: North America

DID YOU KNOW...?

❓ When palaeontologists first found Stenonychosaurus fossils, they thought they belonged to a lizard.

❓ This little dinosaur has suffered a bit of an identity crisis—until 2017, it was called Troodon formosus.

❓ Stenonychosaurus' eyes were larger than those of most modern animals. So it probably had good night vision or hunted in low light, when it was easier to ambush its victims.

COOL CRESTS

DILOPHOSAURUS *(die-LOAF-uh-sore-us)*

- - - ◆ - - -

Dilophosaurus was small compared to the huge meat-eating dinosaurs that followed in its footsteps, but it was the largest predator in North America during the Early Jurassic epoch. It had surprisingly weak jaws, with very long teeth that were more suitable for tearing than biting. Its powerful legs, sharp-clawed feet, and grasping hands were perfect for holding down struggling prey. Dilophosaurus would have been a fast runner and could have reached speeds of 28 miles per hour. The head crests that give it its name were probably used for display or signaling.

 LIVED: 206–194 million years ago

 PERIOD: Early Jurassic

 LENGTH: up to 23 feet

 DIET: smaller animals, including plant-eating dinosaurs, and dead animals

 NAME MEANS: "double-crested lizard" because of its rounded twin crests

Dilophosaurus' twin crests were probably used for display and may have been brightly colored.

LOCATION

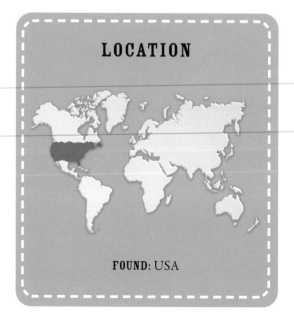

FOUND: USA

DID YOU KNOW...?

❓ Dilophosaurus was one of the first large dinosaur predators. It was about the size of a brown bear.

❓ Several Dilophosaurus fossils were found close together, so they probably lived in small herds or family groups. By hunting as a pack, they would have been able to catch larger prey.

❓ Dilophosaurus' strong legs made up for its lack of jaw power—they allowed it to chase smaller, fast-moving animals. Its four-fingered hands show it was related to Ceratosaurus.

DEVILISH HORNS

CARNOTAURUS *(kah-no-TORE-us)*

- - - ◆ - - -

During the Jurassic period, a large ocean formed between the northern and southern continents, cutting South America off from the north. South American dinosaurs started to develop differently than their northern relatives—while T. rex terrorized plant-eaters in the north, Carnotaurus preyed on those in the south. This southern dinosaur was lighter than T. rex and could run up to 35 miles per hour over short distances. It got its speed from its powerful legs and the large muscles in its tail that helped pull its legs backward when it was running.

 LIVED: 72–70 million years ago

 PERIOD: Late Cretaceous

 LENGTH: up to 29.5 feet

 DIET: fast-moving animals that other, larger predators were too slow to catch

 NAME MEANS: "meat-eating bull" because of its bull-like horns

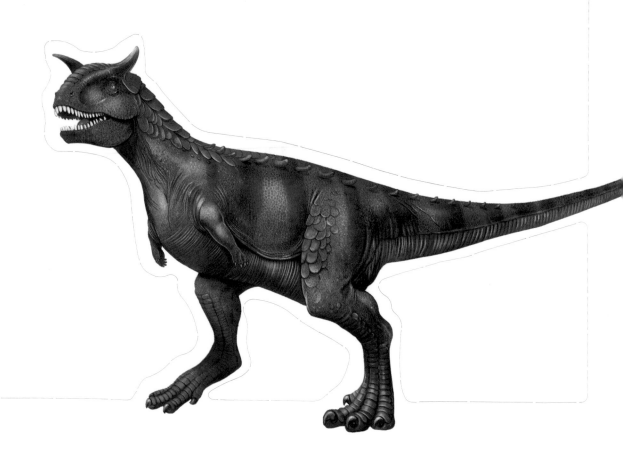

The menacing horns above Carnotaurus' eyes were probably used in battles between rival males.

LOCATION

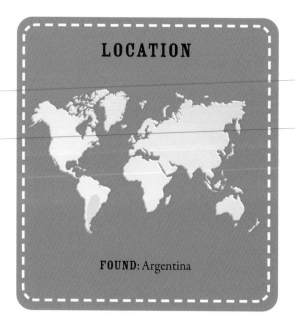

FOUND: Argentina

DID YOU KNOW...?

❷ Tyrannosaurus is known for its small arms, but the arms of Carnotaurus were positively puny. It could not move its fingers and did not have any claws, so they must have been pretty useless.

❷ One fossil of Carnotaurus included impressions of its skin, which was made up of scales with rows of large bumps running along the sides of its neck, back, and tail.

❷ Unlike those of many other dinosaurs, Carnotaurus' eyes faced forward.

SMALL-BRAINED BATTERING RAM

PACHYCEPHALOSAURUS *(pack-ee-KEF-al-uh-sore-us)*

The bony dome protecting this dinosaur's tiny brain was 20 times thicker than a regular dinosaur skull and 30 times thicker than a human one. Scientists believe that rival males used their domed skulls in high-speed, head-butting contests because many skull fossils show signs of old wounds. Others think that the dome was too weak to survive head-to-head clashes, and it was more likely that Pachycephalosauruses locked heads and pushed one another, or rammed each other in the sides. Their short arms and powerful feet show that they walked on two legs.

 LIVED: 76–66 million years ago

 PERIOD: Late Cretaceous

 LENGTH: up to 15 feet

 DIET: probably soft plants, seeds, and fruit because of its tiny, leaf-shaped teeth

 NAME MEANS: "thick-headed lizard" because of its very thick skull

Pachycephalosaurus' domed skull was up to 10 inches thick and was surrounded by bony knobs.

LOCATION

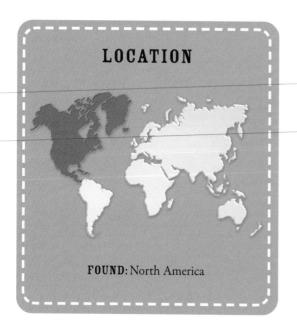

FOUND: North America

DID YOU KNOW...?

❓ All herbivores accidentally eat insects as they munch on leaves, but palaeontologists think Pachycephalosaurus may have actively hunted them.

❓ Pachycephalosaurus may have used its domed head as a defense against predators such as T. rex.

❓ Each species of Pachycephalosaurus had a differently shaped dome on its head. This may have helped them to recognize each other.

MONSTER CLAWS

THERIZINOSAURUS *(THERA-zine-uh-sore-us)*

------ ◆ ------

Therizinosaurus is one of the strangest dinosaurs ever discovered. Its claws measured an incredible 30 inches long—the longest of any known animal. It belongs to the meat-eating group of dinosaurs that includes T rex, so you would expect it to have used its enormous claws as fearsome weapons. Instead, Therizinosaurus was a herbivore and probably used its claws to hook high branches and strip bark from trees. Palaeontologists have yet to find a Therizinosaurus head, so they can only guess at exactly what it ate.

 LIVED: 72–66 million years ago

 PERIOD: Late Cretaceous

 LENGTH: up to 30 feet

 DIET: plants and leaves

 NAME MEANS: "reaping lizard" in Greek because of its scythelike claws

Therizinosaurus is the largest member of this mysterious family of dinosaurs. Fossils show that it may have had feathers at some stage of its life.

LOCATION

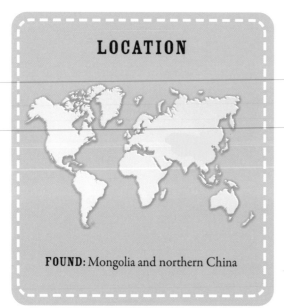

FOUND: Mongolia and northern China

DID YOU KNOW...?

❓ When the first Therizinosaurus bones were found, scientists thought its huge claws belonged to a giant turtle.

❓ It looks like Therizinosaurus lived in groups. A nesting colony with 17 clutches of eggs was found in the Gobi Desert, in Mongolia.

❓ A huge tyrannosaur was also found in Mongolia. Therizinosaurus may have used its claws to defend itself against attacks from this top predator during the Late Cretaceous epoch.

AWESOME EATING MACHINE

MAMENCHISAURUS *(ma-men-chi-SORE-us)*

- - - ◆ - - -

With a neck longer than a school bus, Mamenchisaurus could have plucked leaves from the highest treetops, but instead this sauropod held its head low and swept its neck through the low-growing vegetation like a garden strimmer. This meant it could reach plants in marshy areas that could not support its great weight, and poke its head into gaps between trees that were too narrow for its body to pass through. It fed at the same spot for hours to save energy, but this Jurassic giant still needed more than half a ton of food a day—twice as much as a large elephant!

 LIVED: 160–145 million years ago

 PERIOD: Late Jurassic

 LENGTH: up to 70 feet

 DIET: leaves from low-growing plants

 NAME MEANS: "Mamenchi lizard" after the name of a ferry crossing in China next to the construction site where the first fossil was found

25

Long necks allowed plant-eating dinosaurs to grow to huge sizes because they enabled them to reach food that other animals couldn't.

LOCATION

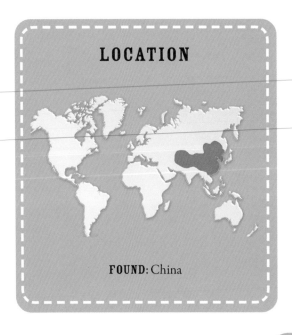

FOUND: China

DID YOU KNOW...?

❓ Mamenchisaurus' neck had an incredible 19 vertebrae (compared to just seven in a giraffe's neck), and it was as long as its body and tail combined.

❓ Scientists think that Mamenchisaurus' heart would not have been strong enough to pump blood all the way up to its head if it was held high.

❓ These Jurassic giants were not just big eaters, they were very thirsty, too—they needed to drink the equivalent of two bathtubs full of water each day.

PINT-SIZED PREDATOR

MICRORAPTOR *(MIKE-row-rap-tur)*

- - - - ◆ - - - -

One of the smallest meat-eating dinosaurs, Microraptor was also one of the strangest. Its front and back legs were covered in long feathers, so it appeared to have four wings. Palaeontologists disagree on whether it could fly or not—it had claws designed for climbing, so it may have climbed into trees and used its feathered limbs to glide down, perhaps flapping its front legs at the same time. It lived in the forests of northeastern China, in an area rich in well-preserved dinosaur fossils—the remains of hundreds of Microraptor have been found there.

 LIVED: 125–120 million years ago

 PERIOD: Early Cretaceous

 LENGTH: up to 3 feet

 DIET: birds, fish, lizards, and small mammals

 NAME MEANS: "little thief" because of its small size and its claws

Microraptor's large eyes suggest that it hunted at night, rather than during the day.

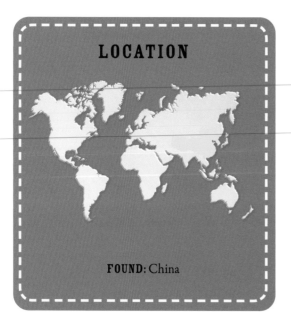

LOCATION

FOUND: China

DID YOU KNOW...?

❓ Microraptor would have been a clumsy ground-walker and easy prey for larger meat-eaters because of its long feathers.

❓ Modern-looking birds already existed during the Cretaceous period, and the bones of a small bird were found in Microraptor's stomach, so it probably preyed on birds roosting or nesting up in the trees.

❓ Similar to a magpie, Microraptor had glossy wings that changed color when seen from different angles.

DAWN OF THE DINOSAURS

EORAPTOR *(ee-oh-RAP-tur)*

Eoraptor was one of the first dinosaurs, and, although small, it has caused a lot of arguments. It was a fast runner and had sharp, pointed teeth, good for preying on small animals. But Eoraptor also had rounded teeth, which are more suited to chewing plants, so it may have been an omnivore. It might look like other small meat-eating dinosaurs of the Jurassic and Cretaceous periods, but certain features suggest that Eoraptor may be more closely related to the giant, long-necked plant-eaters. Some palaeontologists don't think that it was a dinosaur at all!

 LIVED: 231–228 million years ago

 PERIOD: Late Triassic

 LENGTH: 3 feet

 DIET: plants, as well as the remains of dead animals

 NAME MEANS: "eo" is Greek for dawn and "raptor" is Latin for thief because it is one of the earliest small hunters found

Eoraptor ran on its hind legs. It had five-fingered hands with three large claws that it probably used for gripping its prey.

LOCATION

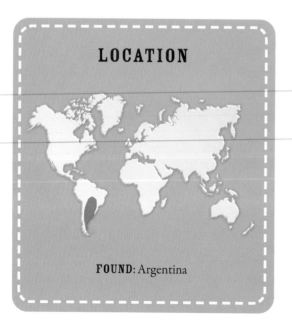

FOUND: Argentina

DID YOU KNOW...?

❓ Because Eoraptor is very different from other dinosaurs, some palaeontologists think it deserves its own special group within the archosaurs. Archosaurs include dinosaurs, pterosaurs, and crocodile-like reptiles.

❓ Despite its name, Eoraptor was not related to any of the raptors of the Cretaceous period, such as Velociraptor.

❓ Eoraptor was found in a place called Valle de la Luna (Valley of the Moon) in Argentina. This stunning fossil site looks like the surface of the Moon.

SUPER-SIZED SKULL

PROTOCERATOPS *(pro-toe-SER-uh-tops)*

Protoceratops was the size of a pig, so it was on the menu for predators both large and small. This did not mean it was defenseless, though. Protoceratops was armed with an impressive set of teeth, plant-shearing jaws, and a parrotlike beak. A fossil unearthed in Mongolia, which was probably preserved by a sudden landslide, proves it did not give up without a fight. It shows Protoceratops and Velociraptor locked in a life-or-death battle. Protoceratops has Velociraptor's arm in its powerful beak, while Velociraptor has one of its killing claws in Protoceratops' throat.

LIVED: 80–71 million years ago

PERIOD: Late Cretaceous

LENGTH: 6 feet

DIET: tough plants

NAME MEANS: "first horned face"—although it had bumps, not horns, on its nose and cheeks

*Protoceratops probably used its
frill to impress rivals and mates.*

LOCATION

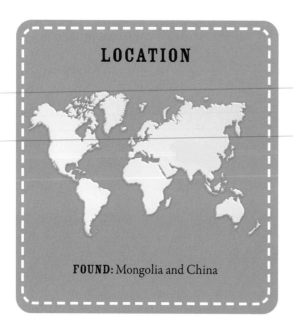

FOUND: Mongolia and China

DID YOU KNOW...?

❓ Protoceratops was related to the much larger Triceratops and Pentaceratops. It traveled in herds, probably as protection against predators.

❓ Protoceratops' skull was huge compared to its body. It needed a big head to house its muscular jaws and large beak.

❓ Protoceratops' teeth were regularly replaced as they wore out. Without its sharp set of teeth, Protoceratops would have starved to death.

EARLY BIRD

ARCHAEOPTERYX *(ark-ee-OP-tuh-rix)*

- - - - ◆ - - - -

The fossil of Archaeopteryx is one of the most important ever found because it shows a link between dinosaurs and modern birds. Archaeopteryx had the wings and feathers of a bird combined with the toothy jaws, clawed fingers, and bony tail of a dinosaur. Studies of its skeleton show that Archaeopteryx probably took flight from the treetops and moved through the air by a combination of gliding and powered flight. True birds evolved during the Late Cretaceous epoch, about 70 million years after Archaeopteryx became extinct.

 LIVED: 150–148 million years ago

 PERIOD: Late Jurassic

 LENGTH: up to 20 inches

 DIET: small reptiles, mammals and insects

 NAME MEANS: "ancient wing," because when it was found it was the oldest known bird

Scientists believe that evolutionary changes that started with gliding from tree to tree led to powered flight in creatures such as Archaeopteryx.

LOCATION

FOUND: Germany

DID YOU KNOW...?

❓ Archaeopteryx had a bigger brain for its size than most dinosaurs. Studies of its brain show that it had keen sight and excellent hearing.

❓ Archaeopteryx remains have been found in what was once a warm lagoon. The sandy bed was perfect for preserving feathers and tiny bones, so although its fossils are rare, they are very detailed and well preserved.

❓ Palaeontologists believe Archaeopteryx may have been able to take flight from a standing start like a modern bird.

SPECTACULAR SAIL

SPINOSAURUS *(SPINE-uh-sore-us)*

---◆---

This mysterious therapod was bigger than T. rex and had tall spines along its back that supported a huge sail. Like a crocodile, Spinosaurus had a long, narrow snout with large, cone-shaped teeth and nostrils high on its skull. This allowed Spinosaurus to breathe with most of its head underwater so it could stay hidden from its prey. It lived in lush, tropical wetlands, where there were few large plant-eaters to prey on, but which were packed with freshwater sharks, huge turtles, and giant fish, including coelacanths, which were the size of a car.

 LIVED: 112–97 million years ago

 PERIOD: mid Cretaceous

 LENGTH: up to 59 feet

 DIET: giant turtles and fish, including coelacanths, sawfish, lungfish, and sharks

 NAME MEANS: "spine lizard" because of the 6.5-foot-long spines on its back

Spinosaurus used its strong arms and clawed hands to catch its prey.

LOCATION

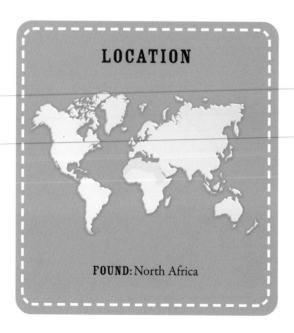

FOUND: North Africa

DID YOU KNOW...?

❓ Most theropods had hollow bones like modern flying birds, but Spinosaurus had heavy, solid bones, like a penguin.

❓ The spines along Spinosaurus' back were connected to one another by skin to form a huge sail.

❓ Spinosaurus may have displayed its sail to look more threatening or to attract a mate.

CARING PARENTS

MAIASAURA *(my-uh-SORE-uh)*

-----◆-----

Fossils of a Maiasaura nesting colony on the shore of an ancient sea in Montana, were the first proof that large dinosaurs cared for their young. One of the nests contained the remains of 15 baby Maiasaura that were about four weeks old when they died. Their legs were not strong enough for them to walk, but their teeth were worn down, showing that their parents had brought them food. Maiasaura weighed as much as a hippo, which meant it was too big to sit on its nest. It probably kept its eggs warm by covering them with plants, as crocodiles do today.

  LIVED: 80–73 million years ago

 PERIOD: Late Cretaceous

 LENGTH: up to 30 feet

 DIET: ferns, conifers, and ginkgoes

(A) NAME MEANS: "good mother lizard" because fossils show it took good care of its young

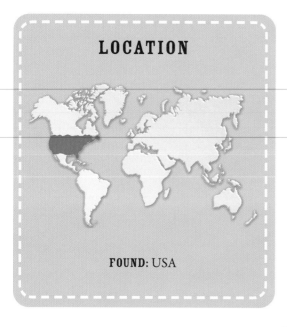

Maiasaura hatchlings spent their early lives in the safety and warmth of a nest, growing bigger and stronger in preparation for adult life.

LOCATION

FOUND: USA

DID YOU KNOW...?

❓ Maiasaura was a duck-billed dinosaur with small, spiky crests in front of its eyes. These were probably used in head-butting contests between rival males and to defend themselves from predators.

❓ Maiasaura lived in large herds and nested together in huge colonies, as some sea birds do today.

❓ Maiasaura laid 30 to 40 eggs in a circular pattern in nests made of earth. These eggs were about the size of ostrich eggs.

MONSTER OF THE DEEP

LIOPLEURODON *(lee-oh-PLOR-uh-don)*

While Allosaurus was terrorizing plant-eating dinosaurs on land, similar battles were taking place beneath the Mesozoic seas. Giant marine reptiles such as mosasaurs, ichthyosaurs, and plesiosaurs were not dinosaurs but they could be every bit as fearsome. Ambush predator Liopleurodon was a pliosaur—a type of plesiosaur—and had one of the biggest skulls of any meat-eater ever to have lived. Its powerful jaws were packed with needle-sharp teeth, and it used its excellent sense of smell to help it track down prey.

 LIVED: 162–153 million years ago

 PERIOD: Middle to Late Jurassic

 LENGTH: up to 23 feet

 DIET: marine reptiles, such as other plesiosaurs, marine crocodiles, ichthyosaurs, and large fish

 NAME MEANS: "smooth-sided teeth" because the first fossils found of this dinosaur were three teeth

Liopleurodon thrust itself through the water using its strong, paddle-shaped limbs, then used its massive jaws and powerful neck muscles to catch its prey.

LOCATION

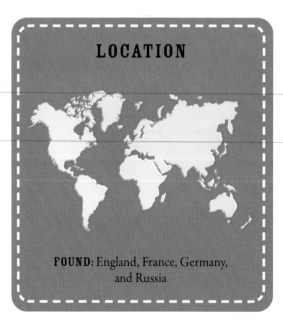

FOUND: England, France, Germany, and Russia

DID YOU KNOW...?

❓ Pliosaurs and other marine reptiles had lungs so they had to surface to gulp air, like modern-day whales and dolphins.

❓ Liopleurodon's massive skull was 5 feet wide, so very few prehistoric sea creatures were too big for it to bite!

❓ The spine bones of some marine reptiles were as big as dinner plates.

SHARP HORNS, HUGE FRILL

PENTACERATOPS *(pen-tah-SER-ah-tops)*

------◆------

Pentaceratops means "five-horned face," but this relative of Triceratops had just three horns—the fourth and fifth were actually sharply pointed cheekbones. Pentaceratops' most remarkable feature was its massive neck frill, edged with little triangular horns. This impressive face furniture was probably enough to scare off predators and may have even been used to attract mates. Pentaceratops was a ceratopsian dinosaur. Members of this group had sharp beaks and rows of cheek teeth for grinding up tough plants.

 LIVED: 76–74 million years ago

 PERIOD: Late Cretaceous

 LENGTH: 20 feet

 DIET: low-growing plants, such as cycads, mosses, and ferns

 NAME MEANS: "five-horned face," although Pentaceratops only had three real horns

41

Pentaceratops had one of the largest heads of any known dinosaur. It was nearly 10 feet from the tip of its beak to the top of its frill.

LOCATION

FOUND: Southern USA

DID YOU KNOW...?

❓ Pentaceratops' neck frill bones had large holes in them, so they were like a frame, supporting tissue and skin. If they had been solid bone, they would have been very heavy.

❓ Pentaceratops' neck frills may have done two jobs, absorbing heat from the sun to keep Pentaceratops warm as well as giving off heat when it got too hot.

❓ Pentaceratops probably lived in herds, like rhinoceroses do today.

FEROCIOUS PACK-HUNTER

DEINONYCHUS *(die-NON-i-kuss)*

Compared to a terrifying tyrannosaur, Deinonychus may not have seemed much of a threat to a large plant-eating dinosaur, but this fast-moving hunter was equipped with a secret weapon. The second toe of each hind foot was armed with a huge, razor-sharp claw. Also, it could move its tail without moving the rest of its body because of a special joint at the base. This helped it balance when it was attacking prey. Teams of these clever raptors attacked from all sides, biting and slashing prey with their claws. Together, they could take down dinosaurs much bigger than themselves.

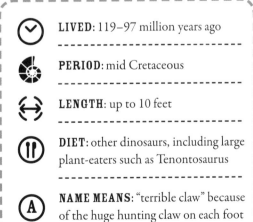

LIVED: 119–97 million years ago

PERIOD: mid Cretaceous

LENGTH: up to 10 feet

DIET: other dinosaurs, including large plant-eaters such as Tenontosaurus

NAME MEANS: "terrible claw" because of the huge hunting claw on each foot

Deinonychus' agility, sharp eyesight, and excellent sense of smell made it a highly effective hunter.

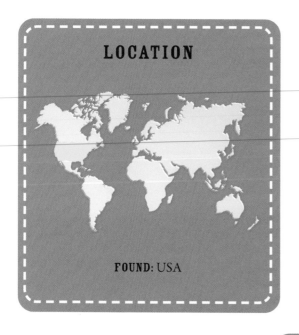

LOCATION

FOUND: USA

DID YOU KNOW...?

❓ Deinonychus had sharp, curved teeth, and its bite was as powerful as an alligator's. Bite marks on a Tenontosaurus skeleton prove that these small raptors could bite through bone and that they must have hunted in packs because Tenontosaurus was many times their size.

❓ Deinonychus lived in warm, swampy forests with lagoons and river deltas.

❓ Palaeontologists think Deinonychus may have had feathers.

MEAN KILLING MACHINE

ALLOSAURUS

(al-uh-SORE-us)

A llosaurus was a fierce hunter that preyed on large plant-eaters. This Jurassic meat-eater had a weaker bite than a lion, but had super-strong skull and neck muscles and could expand its jaws, almost like a snake, to tear huge chunks of flesh from its prey. It may have used its upper jaw like a hatchet, opening its mouth wide and bringing its teeth crashing down on its victim. Fossils indicate a battle between an Allosaurus and a Stegosaurus. Allosaurus' tail bone has a break matching a Stegosaurus tail spike, and the Stegosaurus neck bone shows an Allosaurus-shaped bite.

 LIVED: 155–150 million years ago

 PERIOD: Late Jurassic

 LENGTH: up to 39 feet

 DIET: large herbivores, including Stegosaurus and young sauropods

 NAME MEANS: "different lizard" because its spine was a different shape from any other known dinosaur

Allosaurus had unusual brow horns and ridges of bone in front of each eye. They may have been used for protection and display, or even as weapons.

LOCATION

FOUND: North America, Portugal, and Tanzania

DID YOU KNOW...?

❓ Allosaurus had long, bladelike teeth for slashing and slicing its victims.

❓ Allosaurus' bite was weaker than a lion's or an alligator's, so it probably used its big skull to stun prey.

❓ Big Al, the nickname given to an Allosaurus fossil found in 1991, had lots of broken bones. Paleontologists think these may have been caused by a clash with a Stegosaurus or an Apatosaurus protecting her young.

EARLY GIANT

PLATEOSAURUS *(PLAT-ee-oh-sore-us)*

- - - ◆ - - -

Plateosaurus was one of the first really big dinosaurs. It belonged to a group of long-necked plant-eaters that were the ancestors of the giant Jurassic sauropods, such as Brachiosaurus. During the Late Triassic epoch, the climate was hot and dry, so food could be hard to find. Thanks to its long neck, Plateosaurus was able to reach plants that were too high up for most other dinosaurs to feed on. Supported on its strong back legs, it pulled down branches with its long-clawed hands and tore the leaves off with its sharp teeth.

LIVED: 215–205 million years ago

PERIOD: Late Triassic

LENGTH: 30 feet

DIET: the leaves of conifers, cycads, and tree ferns

NAME MEANS: "broad lizard," but no one knows why it has this name

Plateosaurus walked on its hind legs and used its hands for plucking leaves and pulling down branches. It used its muscular tail as a support.

LOCATION

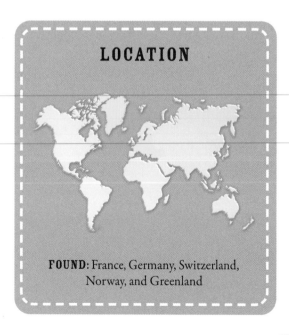

FOUND: France, Germany, Switzerland, Norway, and Greenland

DID YOU KNOW...?

❓ More than 100 well-preserved Plateosaurus skeletons have been found—many at a site in Germany. Scientists think they may have gotten stuck in the mud, or drowned and been washed there after a storm or flood.

❓ Plateosaurus had five-fingered hands with a large thumb claw. This may have been used to collect food, or for defense.

❓ Plateosaurus had a small brain, which suggests it was probably one of the least intelligent dinosaurs.

BATTLE TANK

GASTONIA *(gas-TOH-nee-ah)*

--- ◆ ---

One of the most heavily armored dinosaurs, Gastonia was a match for its main rival, Utahraptor—an ambush predator that stalked the forests of western America in the Early Cretaceous epoch. Its body was shielded by bony plates, and rows of sharp spines ran along its back and sides. Gastonia's tail was a formidable weapon. It could swing it with great force, knocking an attacker off its feet and slashing its flesh with the spikes. A hungry carnosaur could only take a bite out of Gastonia if it had rolled it on its back and attacked its unprotected belly.

 LIVED: 129–122 million years ago

 PERIOD: Early Cretaceous

 LENGTH: up to 16 feet

 DIET: low-growing plants

 NAME MEANS: "Gaston's" because the first fossil was found by Robert Gaston

*Gastonia had short, sturdy legs to support
the weight of its heavily armored body.*

LOCATION

FOUND: USA

DID YOU KNOW...?

❓ Gastonia was an ankylosaur, a group
of slow-moving plant-eaters covered with
bony plates.

❓ Ankylosaurs such as Gastonia had
small brains compared to their body size,
but the area devoted to smell was larger than
usual, so they probably used their noses to
find food.

❓ Gastonia lived in partially forested areas
and probably in herds.

SUPER-SLASHER

GIGANOTOSAURUS *(jig-ah-NO-toe-sore-us)*

— — — ◆ — — —

In the Cretaceous period, Argentina was ruled by record-breaking dinosaurs, and Giganotosaurus is one of the largest land-based carnosaurs discovered. It was armed with bladelike teeth that were perfect for slashing and slicing its prey. Its victims were enormous titanosaurs that shared its habitat. By biting these long-necked plant-eaters on the legs, it wounded them. Then it waited for them to bleed to death. There is evidence that these monster meat-eaters hunted in packs, so the huge, slow-moving herbivores would have had no chance of escape.

LIVED: 98–97 million years ago

PERIOD: mid Cretaceous

LENGTH: 41 feet

DIET: large, plant-eating dinosaurs

NAME MEANS: "giant southern lizard" in Greek

Giganotosaurus had powerful back legs with three sharp talons on its toes and a long tail to help counterbalance its massive skull.

LOCATION

FOUND: Argentina

DID YOU KNOW...?

❓ Giganotosaurus was a carcharodontosaur, a relative of Carcharodontosaurus, whose name means "shark-toothed lizard." They both had super-sharp teeth.

❓ Giganotosaurus' head was as big as a bathtub, with a brain the size of a banana. It could have swallowed a human in one bite.

❓ It appears that Giganotosaurus had a good sense of smell, which would have helped it track down wounded prey as well as dead meat.

LONG-LEGGED SPRINTER

STRUTHIOMIMUS *(STRUTH-ee-oh-mee-mus)*

- - - - ◆ - - - -

Struthiomimus was a champion runner of the Late Cretaceous epoch. Its long and powerful legs could have reached speeds of up to 50 miles per hour. Running was probably its main form of defense, but it may also have defended itself with its strong leg muscles and hind claws. Even though it looked and behaved like a modern ostrich, the two are not related. Birds evolved from small theropods (meat-eating, two-legged, fast dinosaurs with hollow bones), and all Struthiomimus-like dinosaurs became extinct at the end of the Cretaceous period.

 LIVED: 76–70 million years ago

 PERIOD: Late Cretaceous

 LENGTH: up to 13 feet

 DIET: insects, plants, seeds, and small animals

 NAME MEANS: "ostrich mimic" because it was so similar to an ostrich

Struthiomimus had three-fingered hands with sharp claws. Its hands and claws were longer than those of similar dinosaurs, and it probably used them for feeding.

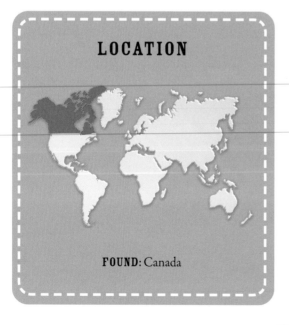

LOCATION

FOUND: Canada

DID YOU KNOW...?

❓ It's possible that Struthiomimus had feathers. It is a close relative of Ornithomimus, and an Ornithomimus fossil showed that it had feathers similar to a modern ostrich.

❓ Struthiomimus had a sharp-edged beak with no teeth, which could have been used for slicing through plants or chopping small animals into bite-sized pieces.

❓ Struthiomimus would probably have used its stiff tail to help it balance when it was running or reaching for food.

WHIPLASH WEAPON

DIPLODOCUS *(DIP-luh-dock-us)*

-------◆-------

Diplodocus was one of the longest animals ever to have walked on Earth, but it was light for its size because it had hollow bones. This huge sauropod laid eggs that were surprisingly small for such a big animal. The newly hatched babies would have made a tasty snack for large predators such as Allosaurus, and hatchlings that survived grew very quickly. Diplodocus herds probably protected their young—their tails were whiplike weapons that could shatter bones and make a terrifying noise as they lashed out at breakneck speeds.

 LIVED: 155–145 million years ago

PERIOD: Late Jurassic

 LENGTH: up to 100 feet

 DIET: conifers and tree ferns

 NAME MEANS: "double beam" because of the two rows of bones that supported its heavy tail

Diplodocus held its neck almost horizontally and grazed on low-growing plants. Its head and brain were small compared to the size of its body.

LOCATION

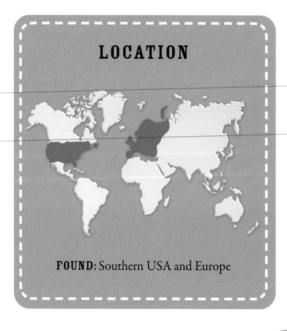

FOUND: Southern USA and Europe

DID YOU KNOW...?

❓ Diplodocus lived alongside giant herbivore Camarasaurus because they ate different plants: Diplodocus used its long, thin teeth to rake up leaves, while Camarasaurus ate tough leaves and branches with its strong, wide teeth.

❓ Diplodocus' incredibly long tail acted as a counterbalance for its far-reaching neck.

❓ Diplodocus had five toes, like other sauropods, but the claw on its "thumb" toe was much bigger than that of its relatives. No one knows what this claw was used for!

MORE BRAWN THAN BRAINS

STEGOSAURUS *(STEG-uh-sore-us)*

- - - - ◆ - - - -

Stegosaurus was the size of a bus. It was the biggest of the plant-eating stegosaurs. It had huge bony plates along its back, smaller ones on its neck, and four bony spikes on the end of its tail. Although this huge dinosaur moved slowly because of its bulk, its size and spiky tail were enough to put off most predators. Its bony plates could be more than 2 feet tall and 2.5 feet wide—that's about half the size of a front door! Each of the four bony spikes on the end of its tail were about three feet long, which is about as long as a guitar.

LIVED: 155–145 million years ago

PERIOD: Jurassic

LENGTH: up to 29.5 feet

DIET: low-growing plants

NAME MEANS: "roof lizard" in Greek because the armored plates on its arched back looked like roof tiles

A strike from one of Stegosaurus' deadly spiked tail weapons could seriously damage or even kill an attacker. Watch out, Allosaurus!

LOCATION

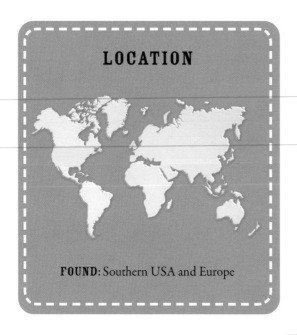

FOUND: Southern USA and Europe

DID YOU KNOW...?

❓ Stegosaurus had 17 bony back plates, which were covered in a network of blood vessels.

❓ As well as controlling body temperature, these plates might have flushed with bright color to scare off predators, attract a mate, or help members of the same species identify each other.

❓ Stegosaurus' brain was very small and probably similar to a hot dog in size as well as shape.

LEGGY LEAF-EATER
BRACHIOSAURUS *(BRAK-ee-uh-sore-us)*

◆

Brachiosaurus was a strange-looking sauropod—its front legs were longer than its hind legs, giving it a sloping back, and its tail was short compared to its neck. This huge dinosaur lived in herds, and each one needed to eat 440 to 880 pounds of plants every day. It had a wide mouth with spoon-shaped teeth that were perfect for stripping leaves from branches but no good for chewing, so it swallowed its food whole. Brachiosaurus was as tall as a four-story building, so it could pluck the juiciest, freshest shoots from the tops of the trees.

 LIVED: 156–144 million years ago

 PERIOD: Late Jurassic

 LENGTH: up to 82 feet

 DIET: the leaves of conifers, ginkgoes, and cycads

 NAME MEANS: "arm reptile" because the length of its upper arm bone was longer than the height of a human

Brachiosaurus had such long legs, a Stegosaurus could have walked underneath its belly.

LOCATION

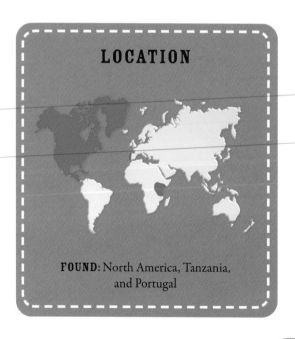

FOUND: North America, Tanzania, and Portugal

DID YOU KNOW...?

❓ Palaeontologists once thought that Brachiosaurus lived in the water and used its nostrils like a snorkel because they were on the top of its head.

❓ In 1991, an asteroid was named after Brachiosaurus.

❓ An adult Brachiosaurus weighed about 15 times more than Allosaurus, so it had little to fear from the top predator of the Late Jurassic epoch, but younger members of the herd would have been at risk of attack.

RULER OF THE SKIES

QUETZALCOATLUS *(ket-zal-koh-AT-lus)*

Quetzalcoatlus was one of the largest known airborne creatures that ever lived. It was a giant reptile known as a pterosaur and it grew to the size of a small plane. Pterosaurs soared above the dinosaurs on wings made from a very strong flap of skin that was supported by one long finger and attached to the side of its body. Rather than flapping its wings and actively flying, Quetzalcoatlus probably glided, using warm up-drafts and breezes to keep itself airborne. Because of its massive wingspan, taking off would have also been difficult.

 LIVED: 70–66 million years ago

PERIOD: Late Cretaceous

 LENGTH: a wingspan of up to 39 feet

 DIET: young dinosaurs, small mammals, amphibians, and fish

 NAME MEANS: "Quetzalcoatl's" because this dinosaur looks like the Mexican feathered snake god, Quetzalcoatl

Quetzalcoatlus had a large brain and big eyes that helped it to spot its prey from the air.

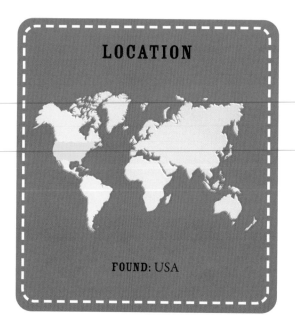

LOCATION

FOUND: USA

DID YOU KNOW...?

❓ Quetzalcoatlus had toothless jaws and a long, thin beak that was longer than the height of an adult human.

❓ These giant pterosaurs had beaks like storks, and they probably hunted in the same way, stalking their prey on the ground or sitting at the edges of streams and rivers snatching food as it swam by.

❓ Quetzalcoatlus was big enough to carry off a human being.